IF FOUND P

👤 _____

✉ _____

📱 _____

Greater Than a Tourist Book Series Reviews from Readers

I think the series is wonderful and beneficial for tourists to get information before visiting the city.

-Seckin Zumbul, Izmir Turkey

I am a world traveler who has read many trip guides but this one really made a difference for me. I would call it a heartfelt creation of a local guide expert instead of just a guide.

-Susy, Isla Holbox, Mexico

New to the area like me, this is a must have!

 -Joe, Bloomington, USA

This is a good series that gets down to it when looking for things to do at your destination without having to read a novel for just a few ideas.

-Rachel, Monterey, USA

Good information to have to plan my trip to this destination.

-Pennie Farrell, Mexico

Great ideas for a port day.

-Mary Martin USA

Aptly titled, you won't just be a tourist after reading this book. You'll be greater than a tourist!

-Alan Warner, Grand Rapids, USA

Even though I only have three days to spend in San Miguel in an upcoming visit, I will use the author's suggestions to guide some of my time there. An easy read - with chapters named to guide me in directions I want to go.

-Robert Catapano, USA

Great insights from a local perspective! Useful information and a very good value!

-Sarah, USA

This series provides an in-depth experience through the eyes of a local. Reading these series will help you to travel the city in with confidence and it'll make your journey a unique one.

-Andrew Teoh, Ipoh, Malaysia

>TOURIST

GREATER THAN A TOURIST- STOCKHOLM SWEDEN

50 Travel Tips from a Local

Alexander Dudley

Greater Than a Tourist- Stockholm Sweden Copyright © 2018 by CZYK Publishing LLC. All Rights Reserved.

All rights reserved. No part of this book may be reproduced in any form or by any electronic or mechanical means including information storage and retrieval systems, without permission in writing from the author. The only exception is by a reviewer, who may quote short excerpts in a review.

The statements in this book are of the authors and may not be the views of CZYK Publishing or Greater Than a Tourist.

Cover designed by: Ivana Stamenkovic
Cover Image: https://pixabay.com/en/royal-palace-sweden-stockholm-377913/

CZYK Publishing Since 2011.

Greater Than a Tourist
Visit our website at www.GreaterThanaTourist.com

Lock Haven, PA
All rights reserved.
ISBN: 9781791868826

>TOURIST
50 TRAVEL TIPS FROM A LOCAL

BOOK DESCRIPTION

Are you excited about planning your next trip?

Do you want to try something new?

Would you like some guidance from a local?

If you answered yes to any of these questions, then this Greater Than a Tourist book is for you.

Greater Than a Tourist- Stockholm, Sweden by Alexander Dudley offers the inside scoop on Stockholm. Most travel books tell you how to travel like a tourist. Although there is nothing wrong with that, as part of the Greater Than a Tourist series, this book will give you travel tips from someone who has lived at your next travel destination.

In these pages, you will discover advice that will help you throughout your stay. This book will not tell you exact addresses or store hours but instead will give you excitement and knowledge from a local that you may not find in other smaller print travel books.

Travel like a local. Slow down, stay in one place, and get to know the people and the culture. By the time you finish this book, you will be eager and prepared to travel to your next destination.

TABLE OF CONTENTS

BOOK DESCRIPTION
TABLE OF CONTENTS
DEDICATION
ABOUT THE AUTHOR
HOW TO USE THIS BOOK
FROM THE PUBLISHER
OUR STORY
WELCOME TO
> TOURIST
INTRODUCTION
1. Airport Shuttle
2. Start With A Healthy Swedish Breakfast
3. Avoid Bringing Cash
4. Try Your Hand At Swedish
5. Enjoy Stockholm's Vegan Options
6. Prepare For An Early Lunch
7. Fika
8. Enjoy 'After Work' Deals
9. The Swedish Spa Experience
10. Take Advantage Of Free Museums
11. Moderna Museet
12. Armémuseum
13. Vasa Museum
14. Experience ABBA

15. Step Back In Time
16. Naturhistoriska Riksmuseet
17. Ways To Get Around
18. Subway Art
19. Djurgården
20. Gamla Stan
21. Urban Södermalm
22. Östermalm
23. Know Your Korv
24. Queuing
25. Summer Time Fun
26. Midsummer
27. Punctuality Is Key
28. Wifi Is Everywhere
29. Small Talk
30. Tap Water
31. Tipping
32. Carry Some Change
33. House Manners
34. Try A Swedish IKEA
35. Life's A Boat
36. Hostels
37. LGBT Friendly
38. Embrace Sweden's Viking History
39. Stay Active
40. Winter Fun

41. Need To Work?
42. Sport In Stockholm
43. Smart Casual
44. Island Hopping
45. Lunch Meal Hacks
46. SkyView Elevator
47. Sea Food Lovers
48. Appropriate Footwear
49. Attending A Weekend House Party?
50. Do The Free Walking Tour

Top Reasons To Book This Trip

Resources

50 THINGS TO KNOW ABOUT PACKING LIGHT FOR TRAVEL

Packing and Planning Tips

Travel Questions

Travel Bucket List

NOTES

DEDICATION

This book is dedicated to my beautiful girlfriend, Felicia. She is my rock and has made the transition into living in a new country easy, as well as a possibility.

My ever supporting mom, dad and brother who have always supported me through everything that I have wanted to do.

Finally, my inspirational grandparents Pearl and Leonard- everything I do is to make them proud.

ABOUT THE AUTHOR

Alexander is a British expat who moved to Sweden after finding love. He has previously travelled and blogged his way across North and South America, as well as Australia, Central America and Europe. He believes the best thing about travelling is learning about cultures from around the world, as well as learning more about yourself.

Upon finishing university at Anglia Ruskin, he jumped into the travelling life, especially travelling solo- because that is the best way to do it. After finishing his first solo trip, he made life-long friends and memories that would last forever. Within weeks he booked up various future trips- including one to Central America.

While in Guatemala he grew close with a Swede. Within six months of this trip ending he visited Sweden for the third time in his life- this time learning of the true beauty and uniqueness of the county. It was on this first trip when he would meet his future girlfriend.

Following text chains and phone calls for five months with Felicia, Alexander decided to take the big jump and commit to moving to Stockholm.

Since then, he has never looked back and has loved every second of living in his new homeland. Uncovering secret gems, leaning the secrets behind the Vikings and taking in all the local cuisine and culture.

He has worked with award winning companies in the Swedish capital such as The Local, American Trails Magazine and Slow Travel Stockholm- making him the ideal person to share his expert tips into how to best experience Stockholm.

>TOURIST

HOW TO USE THIS BOOK

The Greater Than a Tourist book series was written by someone who has lived in an area for over three months. The goal of this book is to help travelers either dream or experience different locations by providing opinions from a local. The author has made suggestions based on their own experiences. Please do your own research before traveling to the area in case the suggested places are unavailable.

Travel Advisories: As a first step in planning any trip abroad, check the Travel Advisories for your intended destination.
https://travel.state.gov/content/travel/en/traveladvisories/traveladvisories.html

FROM THE PUBLISHER

Traveling can be one of the most important parts of a person's life. The anticipation and memories that you have are some of the best. As a publisher of the Greater Than a Tourist book series, as well as the popular 50 Things to Know book series, we strive to help you learn about new places, spark your imagination, and inspire you. Wherever you are and whatever you do I wish you safe, fun, and inspiring travel.

Lisa Rusczyk Ed. D.
CZYK Publishing

OUR STORY

Traveling is a passion of the "Greater than a Tourist" series creator. Lisa studied abroad in college, and for their honeymoon Lisa and her husband toured Europe. During her travels to Malta, an older man tried to give her some advice based on his own experience living on the island since he was a young boy. She was not sure if she should talk to the stranger but was interested in his advice. When traveling to some places she was wary to talk to locals because she was afraid that they weren't being genuine. Through her travels, Lisa learned how much locals had to share with tourists. Lisa created the "Greater Than a Tourist" book series to help connect people with locals. A topic that locals are very passionate about sharing.

>TOURIST

WELCOME TO
> TOURIST

>TOURIST

INTRODUCTION

"We live in a wonderful world that is full of beauty, charm, and adventure. There is no end to the adventures we can have if only we seek them with our eyes open."

– Jawaharial Nehru

When I first visited Stockholm back in 2014 I was visiting as a tourist and was eager to visit all the sights. This was when I first found out about this unique city. The laid back approach of the Swedes, the beautiful scenery- I just wanted to cover every inch of this wonderful city. Stockholm is unlike any other city in the world when it comes to efficiency; especially in the case of their public transport. However, the over-riding factor whenever I think about my first trip to the capital was just how much I still had to experience. There are an abundance of hidden gems, more than any other city in Europe.

Stockholm is the largest city in the whole of Scandinavia and had long been on my radar as a place to visit- in no small part down to my Nan's love for a certain Swedish band. But there is more to the city than national treasures such as ABBA, IKEA and Zlatan Ibrahimovic.

While it's true that Stockholm is indeed one of the most expensive places in Europe to visit and live, the history that comes pouring out of this magical city makes it a cool place to come.

Vikings and a royal family that stretches back centuries are certain places to start. The narrow alleys of the medieval quarter in 'Gamla Stan' are unforgettable, while you can experience palaces, kingdoms and famous buildings equally on water by ferries or on land by foot.

On your journey through Stockholm's past and present you will experience all 14 islands and 50 bridges that ensures Stockholm more than lives up to its tag of 'beauty on water'.

My massive surprise came on the evenings. This is where the city really comes alive and becomes a hub of liveliness and cosmopolitan spirit. The nightlife is trendy and exciting, something that isn't typical of all Nordic cities.

That in a nutshell is what makes Stockholm so special- it is everything that you expect plus much more, it exceeds any expectation that you have.

>TOURIST

1. AIRPORT SHUTTLE

There are four airports scattered around the city- Bromma, Skavsta, Arlanda and Västerås. All of which have different incoming and outgoing flights dependant on where you are flying from. Chances are, if you enter Sweden from outside of Europe you will arrive at Arlanda, as that is the main airport in Stockholm. Meanwhile, if you arrive from mainland Europe it could be any of those choices. Västerås is the smallest of the four and only has two incoming and two outgoing flights a day. There is also no other option except the shuttle to get back and forth from the airport.

However, should you fly into any of the other three airports; you would be best suited to looking at local transport before booking onto a shuttle. Of course, dependant on the time that you arrive into Sweden- the shuttles from the airport tend to be the most expensive route into the city.

This is especially the case when exiting Arlanda airport. You simply follow signs towards the local bus terminal, and search for the one that goes to Märsta station. This is a commuter rail line- the whole route to the T-Centralen (Stockholm's central station) can be covered on a single ticket, which would cost

$3. Swedes do make life even easier for you as you can simply download the SL travel app and book your tickets on there.

2. START WITH A HEALTHY SWEDISH BREAKFAST

Most Swedes tend to enjoy their breakfast before heading out to work or school, but that doesn't mean that there is a lack of places to eat what they call 'the most important meal of the day' within Stockholm.

Breakfast flavors are generally mild. You can always expect to see freshly brewed coffee on the table- it is most Swedish people's first thought in the mornings. Yoghurt, dairy products and cereals are other common foods around the table. Compared to most countries, their breakfast habits are a lot healthier, Swedes in general are very healthy people and would often be seen eating fruit or drinking fruit juice as they walk as opposed to chocolate and fizzy drinks.

People's habits would be dependent on the person. Some might be happy taking a simple cup of coffee and hold on until the 10:00am fika at work.

>TOURIST

Nybrogatan 38 is a good starting point for those who are looking for freshly baked croissants and classic Swedish knäckebrödon (type of cracker). However, if healthy options aren't for you or you are travelling on a budget, then check out the Greasy Spoon in Södermalm.

3. AVOID BRINGING CASH

Sweden is a step ahead of most countries when it comes to its payment, most small businesses such as coffee shops and bars will only accept card and cash will be nowhere in sight.

This is a strange aspect to get used to when you're brought up paying for everything in cash but in Sweden, as my girlfriend says "only people over the age of 60 carry cash anymore."

Of course, you should still bring a little amount of Swedish Krona but not too much, as you will also struggle to exchange it- especially in Sweden.

This is additionally difficult for those that visit Stockholm as many banks ensure that you pay charges once you pay for an item in a different currency. The best advice on this front would be to ensure you have a fully loaded Cash Passport.

Additionally, if you're looking to move to Stockholm for good, it isn't difficult to open a bank account. All you need is a job contract and your passport.

4. TRY YOUR HAND AT SWEDISH

Make no mistake about it; Swedish is an incredibly difficult language to learn. Swedes acknowledge that and are always very friendly when you attempt to speak their language- before then speaking perfect English to clear up any confusion.

You can say hello or goodbye with just 'hej' or 'hej hej' (where the 'j' is pronounced like an English 'y') and 'tack' means both thank you and please, so it's extra easy to be polite.

But fear not, Swedes are well-known for their English skills and speak it at near (if not) native level. You will hear and see English all around you in

>TOURIST

Stockholm. But still, if you would like to try your hand at Swedish, it is easy to do with minimal effort.

Swedish Phrase & English Translation

Hey (HAY) Hello

Hur mår du? (Hoor moor doo?) How are you?

Snälla. (SNELL-la) Please

Tack. (TOCK) Thank you

Var så god. (VAHR sha good) You're welcome

Hej då. (Hay doo) Goodbye

5. ENJOY STOCKHOLM'S VEGAN OPTIONS

As I mentioned before, Stockholm is a very healthy and modern city- meaning that there is an abundance of options should you have certain dietary requirements, or purely looking for a clean-eating week.

The vegan offerings around the city are unrivalled. You can order coffee with oat, almond or soya milk in most cafes, get delicious vegan ice cream in stores or at certain take-away spots. You can even try vegan pulled pork (oomph) in fast food chain Max Burger, Vigårda and many other burger restaurants.

Stikki Nikki is the finest vegan establishment in the city and can be found in Södermalm. They produce some of the finest ice cream in the city, not to mention it is all created organically and made with the freshest of ingredients. It is my personal favorite place to get ice cream in the whole city.

6. PREPARE FOR AN EARLY LUNCH

If breakfast is the most important meal of the day then lunch is the biggest. Many Stockholm restaurants typically offer buffet lunches with a fixed price and start service at noon. However, if you're looking to appease a sweet tooth, you will be looking in the wrong place as that is what the Swedish fika is about.

Swedish lunch also typically means a proper cooked meal, which means having enough time to be able to enjoy it.

>TOURIST

Swedish law ensures that elementary schools provide meals to all pupils free of charge, while pre-schools and secondary schools also follow the same guidelines.

Adults in the workplace rarely have the luxury of a lunch provided free of charge by an employer, and instead have to choose whether to spend part of their weekend cooking up boxed meals for the working week or head out to a restaurant. The secondary is the popular option, as previously mentioned most restaurants have lunch specials at a favourable price.

7. FIKA

You have probably already read this word a few times through this book so far, but now you will learn what it means- it's the Swedes favorite time of the day.

Fika is simply stopping your day to have a coffee and a piece of cake. It is popular all around the city; with every work place taking at least one fika break a day. Typically there would be a break at 10:00 or 16:00 for this. It is dependent on the work place- it could even be both.

Sweden enjoys a highly developed culture when it comes to baked good, and everywhere in Stockholm, you will find cafes and cake shops that are full of atmosphere and character.

8. ENJOY 'AFTER WORK' DEALS

When it comes to the nightlife, as you could imagine it is expensive. Most people that live in Stockholm tend to go out once a month for a good night out. However, most bars will be busy from 16:00 as that is when drinks in bars have discounted prices.

'After Work' hours tend to differ on where you go but are generally between 16:00 and 18:30. Many pubs will serve a cheaper drink between these hours. There is even a club, 'Out of Office', that kicks off in the late afternoon instead of late evening and they cater towards thirsty office workers.

You can download their official app for your free entrance ticket and be prepared to dance your suit off.

>TOURIST

9. THE SWEDISH SPA EXPERIENCE

Nudity is something that I- as a Brit, have always been taught is something that is only for private. However, Swedes do not follow those same rules and their spas just show you that.

The Nordic ritual is to strip down in the sauna. Don't expect to bring anything but yourself and a towel, which is mostly for drying yourself off after you plunge into an ice lake.

I think this is a great sign of how cool the Swedish are, and is something that I have grown to love while living here.

If you're looking to do a spa day which you're in Stockholm, the obvious choice is Sparadiset. It's a slice of heaven and the service by all staff throughout your day is excellent. However, don't expect it to be cheap, no spa experiences in Stockholm are cheap and a considered a luxury.

10. TAKE ADVANTAGE OF FREE MUSEUMS

There is history wherever you look in Stockholm, but the best way to see history in any country is by visiting a museum. Stockholm has an array of museums scattered around the city with each establishment offering something different.

You can choose to see the best preserved warship from the 17th century or explore the first open air museum in the country. However, if you would prefer seeing contemporary art or learn of old history, there is a museum for everyone.

Additionally, it makes it even better that some of the best ones are free.

Yes, they are free. No charge to get into some of the museums- however, some of the areas would indeed take a charge but I shall take you through some of the best free museums that you have to visit.

>TOURIST

11. MODERNA MUSEET

The Moderna Museet in Stockholm is one of the leading museums in Europe for modern and contemporary art.

Here you can experience the best of art from the twentieth century to today, featuring work from Picasso, Dali and Matisse. The museum is located on Skeppsholmen Island so you're guaranteed to be wowed by the scenery as much as the art inside the museum.

There are more than 130,000 pieces of work located here. They are separated into three categories- Swedish and Nordic art, French-orientated modernism and American art from the 1950 and 60s. Recently they have added a ground-breaking mew collection dedicated to 20th and 21st century women artists and works from a globalised world. Additionally their photography collection is incomparable.

The Moderna Museet Collection is free of charge, however if you would like to see the temporary exhibitions; there will be an admission price.

12. ARMÉMUSEUM

The Swedish Army Museum is one of the best historical museums in the city with three floors full of unique exhibitions and it is free. You will follow men, women and children on their journey through war time in Sweden, beginning in the 1500's and ending at present day. There are fascinating stories told within the museum and they are presented in a special way so they connect with all visitors. The Museum also plays host to a variety of historical objects, only further setting the scene of the living conditions that Swedes in this time period lived in, no matter whether they were a soldier, woman or child.

Armémuseum is smartly able to tell the stories of all classes throughout war time in Sweden. It is a brilliant family day out for educational and enjoyment purposes, with the 'Children's Trail' keeping your little ones busy for hours.

>TOURIST
13. VASA MUSEUM

The Vasa Museum plays host to the only preserved 17th century ship in the entire world. The ship sank on its first voyage from Stockholm Harbor in 1628. Since its recovery in 1961 it has been restored to its former glory for the whole of the country and visitors to see.

Almost the entirety of the ship is original, but don't be entering expecting to walk aboard the famous ship. The closest you can get is being able to walk around the sides of it, at a safe distance. This ensures that you can see every inch of the ship and admire its full beauty. This is the most visited museum in the whole of Scandinavia, and you can learn all about what it was like living on the seas in the 17th century with artifacts also well preserved.

This is not one of the free museums in the city but nonetheless it is a must do. Check their website for the latest prices.

14. EXPERIENCE ABBA

ABBA are the most famous Swedish export, with fans from all around the world touched by their music. However, the museum attracts both fans of the band and general music fanatics. The most enjoyable factor of the museum is its interactive elements; you can dance along to 'Waterloo' or 'Dancing Queen', while also learning the story behind the music.

All members of the band have donated memorabilia and told their stories to enhance the museums originality, while Björn Ulvaeus is also named as Director for the museum and has recently had a massive part in the opening of their latest exhibition, which follows the band members following their separation. It really wraps up the story and the museum now has the complete story from start to present day.

You should buy your tickets well in advance as it is massively popular and queues are common.

>TOURIST

15. STEP BACK IN TIME

Skansen Open Air Museum is the first museum of its kind to open in Sweden. It was first unveiled in 1891 with the primary aim of showing the way of life in the country prior to the industrial revolution. It is most commonly the first museum that visitors want to see, but it is also equally popular with locals- especially during the summer holidays.

Apart from the open air museum, there is also a zoo which plays host to a range of animals that are native to the Scandinavian region, with frequent shows open to the public throughout the day. The museum can be found near Royal Djurgården. The best time to visit is undoubtedly over the summer as the majority of the day will be spent outdoors, you can also see breathtaking views of the whole city from all sides during the summer months. You should definitely stop by and take a step back in time, with over 150 farms and dwellings to see.

16. NATURHISTORISKA RIKSMUSEET

The Swedish Royal Museum of Natural History is one of the two major museums of natural history in Sweden, with the other one is in Gothenburg.

Here you can experience nine permanent exhibitions about nature and the developments of mankind. It is one of the best museums in Stockholm that combines education and enjoyment; and it is a must if you have children. The two most popular exhibitions are the 'Human Journey' which follows the development of humans from seven million years ago to today. The second most popular is the 'Fossil and Evolution' exhibit, just look for the dinosaurs.

The Cosmonova IMAX theatre is another vital point of interest, here you can enter the 760- square meter dome and watch the featured movie. The main museum is free to enter but Cosmonova costs 120 SEK for adults and 80 SEK for children.

>TOURIST
17. WAYS TO GET AROUND

Getting around Stockholm is easy, so fear not if you are a solo traveler. If you are in the city for one week or more it would be worth the money in investing in an SL card. You can frequently top this card up to pay for all your journeys, no matter whether it is used on the bus, train or ferry. You can also get 24-hour and 72-hour passes if you are in Stockholm for shorter than a week.

There are three main Tunnelbana (train) lines: green, red and blue. These connect all the main neighborhoods in Stockholm and trains often leave stations every ten to 15 minutes. Times may vary later on in the evening, weekends and red days (bank holidays). T-Centralen is the main line where everything revolves around.

Ferries are not only an amazing way to see the city but also an efficient way of getting around. There are some useful city lines than ensure island hopping is easy. There are year-long Djurgården ferry shuttles between Slussen and Djurgården. Additionally, the Sjövägen 80 boat line connects central Nybroplan with Frihamnen in an almost-circular loop, stopping at Allmänna Gränd on Djurgården along the way.

This route is the best if you want a short-cut from the downtown area to the museums on Djurgården.

If you're looking to get t an area in the suburbs, the best transport is the bus. There is dozens of lines across the city. Busses in Stockholm are unlike most busses in the world in the fact that they are clean, well maintained and reliable- even if it's snowing.

18. SUBWAY ART

Many of the tourists and locals around Stockholm are oblivious to the works of art that surround them when they are commuting around the city. Touted at the world's longest art exhibition at 110km long, you will find a variety of paintings, sculptures and mosaics among others displayed in the Stockholm subways.

The art is put together by 150 artists and you will see designs in over 90 of the city's 100 stations.

Kungsträdgarden would be the best place to start; here you will see dramatic installations of vibrantly colored abstract harlequin design that engulfs the caves.

>TOURIST

From here you can move onto the main artery of T-Centralen, before then visiting Hötorget, Stadshagen and Solna Centrum.

19. DJURGÅRDEN

One of the city's most beloved islands is loved by Stockholmers and visitors alike. It is a city oasis located in the middle of Stockholm; for good reason as there is nowhere else in Sweden like it.

There is a mixture of all the most famous museums and culture attractions with green nature, parks and family-friendly activities. On this island you will find the Vasa Museum, Gröna Lund and Skansen.

Djurgården can be reached by bus, tram or ferry from T-Centralen. Although Djurgården is beautiful all year round, the summer time is when it really comes alive. The walk along Strandvägen, from the Royal Dramatic Theatre to Djurgårdsbron is my personal favorite route.

20. GAMLA STAN

Simply put, this is the old town and is full of sights, restaurants, cafes and bars. Additionally, it is the perfect place to pick up all your souvenirs. The narrow, winding cobble-stone streets takes you back in time, but the dazzling colors bring you right back, but it all adds to Gamla Stan's unique character.

Västerlånggatan and Österlånggatan are the district's main streets, but be sure to head off the beaten track to get the true feeling of the old town. There are several beautiful museums and attractions here, The Royal Palace being the main attraction.

Lately, Gamla Stan has become a virtual gastro-island, with quite a few excellent and award-winning restaurants to choose from.

21. URBAN SÖDERMALM

Historically this neighborhood used to be a working-class haven but nowadays it is a top hipster neighborhood. You will find all the cool cats around here, as this neighborhood now plays host to independent shops, cafes and bars.

>TOURIST

The spectacular views of the city are an obvious drawing point for the area but the cozy 16th century architecture keeps you gripped.

If you're fan of trendy vintage clothing shops or cool independent galleries and intimate bars, Söder will be your favorite island in Stockholm. It is a wonderful advertisement for modern Stockholm. However, if you aren't a fan of hipsters, bushy beards or Buddy Holly spectacles, this neighborhood won't be your place.

22. ÖSTERMALM

If Södermalm wasn't for you, then Östermalm may be more for you. It is an upper class neighborhood but is beautifully elegant. It has the highest concentration of nightclubs in the city, found around Stureplan.

Additionally, here you will find the best place for shopping. Bibliotekstan is the cities most affluent shopping district, with exclusive Scandinavian and international brands on offer.

The Östermalmshallen is a must while you're here. It is the best food market in the entire city and has an array of all meats, fish and vegetarian options. The perfect spot for lunch in Stockholm, but keep an eye out for celebrities.

Once you've finished lunch, take a walk along Strandvägen to enjoy Östermalm in all its glory of magnificent buildings and fabulous seaside views.

23. KNOW YOUR KORV

When you think of Swedish food you would be forgiven for thinking of meatballs, but Swedes are particularly fond of their korv.

Simply put, Falukorv is a sausage, a big sausage, that Swedes normally slice and eat cold or pan fried. The korv is normally beef and pork buy horse meat is also allowed but rarely used.

However, it's not something you'll find to be frequent in restaurants. It is cheap and usually eaten at home.

>TOURIST

Due to my girlfriends heritage from Dalarna, I am fair too familiar with the history of the falukorv. It dates back to the 16th and 17th century in the regional town of Falun. The town was historically a big copper mining industrial area, which made ropes out of ox hide. That meant there was access to meat which was often salted and smoked. The Lyoner sausage (from Germany) was used as an inspiration and created the falu sausage.

Decades later and the Swedes still go crazy about korv and are considered a must-have in every Swedish household.

24. QUEUING

This is a pretty big thing in the whole of Sweden, not just Stockholm. Everything is organized and the public transport is no different. You often queue for one direction and everyone follows in suit. If you queue from the opposite side, don't expect anyone to let you in.

If you happy to jump the queue, Swedes will be irritated and although they don't like confrontation, they will give you dirty looks and just generally look disapproving.

Bus stations are the main place to remember this tip as this is when the Swedes tend to get more annoyed, mainly because they have just finished a hard day at work, so who wouldn't be annoyed?

Typically lines are formed to the right of the bus door, don't forget.

25. SUMMER TIME FUN

There are very few places that are as beautiful as Sweden in the summer time. The days are at their longest point in the whole year and mood picks up and everyone is happier. My girlfriends main tip for knowing when it's the summer is that bus waiting busses are finally put out- as in the winter you just have to stand there.

Parks become busy and are used as sunbathing areas, you'll need to get there early if you wish to get a space however as they are popular. This is also the case with beer gardens, in the summer time Swedes

>TOURIST

love to sit outside and make the most of the sunshine, who doesn't?

Shorts are frequently worn, even by those that work in the city. The summer time is my favorite part of living in Sweden, the ability to sit outside for the entire summer, with temperatures ranging between 25 and 30 degrees Celsius, it is heavenly.

Swimming in the lakes is also common place during the summer months, the water isn't the warmest but it certainly cools you down after being in the hot weather throughout the day. A must.

However, be aware of the downtime period during the summer. Swedes take their holidays very seriously— normally, by disappearing off to their countryside cottages or island retreats on the archipelago. This means that at certain times of the year, Stockholm is a bit of a ghost town, especially after Midsummer in June and July. On the plus side, visitors get the city to themselves.

26. MIDSUMMER

Midsummer is my favourite time of the year. Celebrated between the 20th and 25th June, this holiday is considered on the same level as Christmas by many Swedes- some even consider it the most important holiday of the year.

The never-ending lunch party involves having flowers in your hair, dancing around poles and singing songs while drinking unsweetened and flavoured schnapps. This will be mainly to wash down the pickled herring that is served with delightful new potatoes, chives and sour cream.

At the centre of the traditional celebrations is the maypole, in Swedish called the Midsommarstången. And if you were thinking there's something rather phallic about a tall pole with two large hoops at the top, that's sort of the point -- many people believe it originated as a symbol of fertility.

The peak of the festivities sees the Swedes imitate frogs, hopping around the maypole while singing the classic tune 'Små grodorna' (The small frogs), which describes frogs in detail, although incorrectly.

>TOURIST

The final key to a successful Midsummer are strawberries. For traditionalists, they absolutely have to be Swedish. This results in months of press coverage about the state of the strawberry harvest.

Ideally, the perfect way to experience an authentic Midsummer is by celebrating at a Swedes house, but there are various parties scattered around the city with the biggest being at Skansen Open Air Museum. A public park would also be suitable; being outdoors is the main factor.

27. PUNCTUALITY IS KEY

The Swedes are efficient in everything that they do. If they say that they are going to meet you at 19:00, they mean that is the latest that they are going to be. But also don't be too early, it's a very tight line that you need to walk on.

I once had a job interview scheduled for 13:30, I got there for 13:00 and the employer was shocked that I turned up that early. She expressed that normally applicants would show up 15 minutes before an interview and that was a good enough time to express interest in the job and also acknowledging that they won't be late.

The most important occasion to remember this is when you are catching a bus, they are rarely late and often arrive on the second that it is advertised.

28. WIFI IS EVERYWHERE

Stockholm is one of the most connected cities in the whole world, almost everywhere you go will have wifi available and it is always free of charge and passwords are a rarity.

This is in no small part down to the amount of phone usage by Swedes, you will never see a Swede riding the subway without at least one headphone in their ear or playing a game on their phone. Along with this, since most Swedes commute to work in Stockholm, the train and bus routes offer a perfect chance to catch up on work or emails.

The longer bus journeys also offer wifi and it is free of charge and much better than you would expect. However, users would have a weekly allowance that

>TOURIST

they can use to ensure that you aren't simply watching video after video, therefore making sure that the wifi continues to operate at a quick speed for all commuters.

29. SMALL TALK

Swedes don't like to be bothered while they are commuting or at any stage to be frank. This means that small talk is off the table, so don't expect to have a chat with a local while you're waiting for your bus or train.

Even when they finish work and head to the local bars for after work drinks, it's very rare that any Swede would head out by themselves, as they know that they will be sitting there by themselves with nobody to talk to.

Try not to make eye contact either because Swedes often think that this is rude and will think that there is something wrong with you. Although, if you are looking at them they might also think that you have a problem with them.

I tend to think this is mainly a problem for Swedish people towards fellow Swedes, as since living in Sweden a lot of locals have spoke to me because as they would say 'you don't look Swedish.' As much as they don't like small talk, they do love meeting new people in their country who aren't Swedish, as they are obsessed with accents. This is especially the case with Swedes who have a good level of English and want to show it off.

30. TAP WATER

Living in Birmingham, England for the majority of my life has taught me that tap water can be good, and luckily for me, this is also the case around Stockholm.

Tap water is delicious in Stockholm and is drinkable, while also being much better quality than most bottled water you can buy from stores. Swedes take an enormous amount of pride in how good their tap water is- something that I can appreciate.

That would be your one step stop to get into Swede's good books within minutes of meeting you, compliment the quality of their tap water and they will love you.

>TOURIST

31. TIPPING

The tipping culture isn't as prominent in Sweden as it is within the UK and USA, so you can have a great meal and avoid paying the extra 10% on tipping the waiters.

Mainly this is down to the extremely good wages that restaurant and bar workers receive in Stockholm (typically around $15 an hour) and therefore the employees able to make a good living without gaining the tips.

However, if you would like to tip for good service, it is always well received. The simple rule is to round the price to the nearest round number- so if a meal comes to 280 SEK, pay 300 SEK. Like I mentioned before, if you don't leave a tip then the staff would still be friendly, but if you give a few kronor's extra it is a good way of saying thank you.

The one place where I would encourage you to tip would be in the bars. Mainly down to the fact that as soon as you tip you would often jump into the front of the queue when there are longer waits, always a positive when the bars are frequently busy during after work hours.

32. CARRY SOME CHANGE

While I previously said that you shouldn't bring too much cash with you, it is also important that you have a little change on you, especially when commuting through the subways.

This is mainly down to the fact that should you need to use the restroom, you will need to pay. Although they are not expensive (20 SEK) it is easier to pay with change as the barriers have change holders.

They don't take cards at these machines, so if you have a weak bladder- change is a must.

33. HOUSE MANNERS

Swedish house manners are very unique and are unlike any other country in the world. There is certain protocol such as not showing up early, but also not too late. This typically Swedish as if you show up early the house won't ready.

Also, the main one that I found was the no shoes in the house. This puts extra emphasis on socks and a lot of Swedes buy cool socks that match their outfit. I had never put that much thought into socks prior to this, so when I went to my first Swedish house party and my girlfriend said to me to wear good socks, I was in total confusion.

Within minutes of being at the party I could understand what she meant and my sock collection is now a lot more extensive than it previously was.

Additionally, the pre-party is an important part of the evening. The best way to do this is to gather together with friends while you get ready, having a few drinks to ease your way. But don't get drunk before you head out.

34. TRY A SWEDISH IKEA

IKEA has become an important part of Sweden's identity abroad and the flat-pack furniture giant now has more than 300 stores around the world. However, the biggest one of them is still rightly in Sweden.

It's located just outside Stockholm, around 15km southwest of the city centre at Kungens Kurva. Some would say that you haven't experienced Sweden properly until you've paid it a visit.

Thankfully there's a completely free bus that will whizz you from central Stockholm to the big blue-and-yellow warehouse in 20 minutes flat.

35. LIFE'S A BOAT

Stockholm is a wonderful city on land but take nothing away from it, on water is really where you see Stockholm and Sweden's beauty in its full force.

Boat trips are a wonderful idea regardless of whether you are travelling with your family, with friends or by yourself. You will have a dozen chances for photos with picturesque scenery no matter on what trip you decide to take.

The Archipelago Tour is a perfect selection if you are looking to experience that untouched nature of unique

>TOURIST

archipelago in Stockholm but only have a short amount of time in the city.

The Djurgården Ferry is a much shorter and less time consuming idea but nethertheless it is a fun way to get to Djurgården. Simply hop on the passenger ferry at Slussen at the southern end of the Old Town and enjoy the eight minute journey to Allmanna Grand by the Gröna Lund Amusement park.

Lake Malar (Mälaren in Swedish) is the third largest freshwater lake in Sweden with an area of over 1,000km2 and a depth of 64m. It spans over 120 kilometres from east to west. There is no better way to explore this area than by boat, and with excursions daily it's almost impossible to resist.

36. HOSTELS

Stockholm hostels have a reputation for innovative design. Not only does each of them have their own richly intriguing history, they will also save you a fortune whether you are only staying for a weekend or a week- a much better option than splashing the cash on the over-expensive hotels.

Af Chapman is a fantastic choice. You can wake up on the water to breathtaking views of Stockholm. It's a classic old boat that has been anchored at Skeppsholm since 1937, but now plays host to over 136 beds. The ship is over 100 years old but it still boasts its charm and this is often overlooked as you walk down its dark corridors with low ceilings.

My personal favorite is Långholmen's Youth Hostel. Here, you will stay in an original renovated prison cell of the Crown Remand Prison (Kronohäktet.) Kronohäktet was built in the 1840's but was closed in 1975. You stay in 2-4 bed cells that are a whole lot more comfortable than they were in the 1800's, but don't fear; you will have your own key! The prison buildings were falling into decay only a short while ago and a lot of hard work ensured. The main core of the building remained. In 1989, the hostel was re-opened after its redevelopment.

37. LGBT FRIENDLY

Sweden- more than any other country in Europe- is known for its progressive values and they're on full display in Stockholm. Their inclusivity travels through hotels, bars and restaurants. Plus,

>TOURIST

Stockholm's Pride celebration is the biggest in Scandinavia and is not to be missed.

Floating bar-restaurant Mälarpaviljongen will be putting on different events throughout the week, including DJ sessions. It is a party that the whole city embraces- making it the best in Europe.

The bar is a hot-spot all year round for the LGBT community, something that is clearly embraces. Along with offering stunning views of the capital, you can also purchase a 'yes way to rose.' Every purchase of this drink at the bar sees a donation made to the Rainbow Fund- a project to help protect the rights of people across the world no matter of their sexual orientation, gender or expression.

38. EMBRACE SWEDEN'S VIKING HISTORY

Is there any better way of learning of Sweden's rich heritage than going back in time? The best Viking village that you haven't heard of is less than 30 minutes away from Stockholm, just outside of Norrtalje.

Storholmen is a non-profit open air museum that includes live actors playing different roles in the closest real-life scenario you could get to life in Sweden during the Viking age.

I spent the afternoon there over the summer and I was amazed to see that the visitor experience is far greater than just being an observer. Instead, you really are a part of what is happening around you. Storholmen pride themselves on giving the visitor a rich and ingenious experience of the Viking age and to leave with the knowledge and appreciation of what the age was like for everyone involved; whether a slave, housewife or a Viking themselves.

The museum is separated by four different pillars: school activities, guided tours, and open days with activities for families and feasts and events with groups. The museum is continuing to grow with new buildings and infrastructure being erected year on year, only heightening the level of experience that the visitor gets.

During the summer, Storholmen becomes a hub for international visitors when people from around the world gather to work together. The village pride themselves on the work they do with a peace

>TOURIST

organization called International Arbetslag (IAL.) This is the Swedish branch of the international peace organization, Service Civil International (SCI.)

The village really comes alive over the summer and friends are made for life. Storholmen is sure to continue its popularity so be sure to check it out.

Aifur Krog & Bar and Vikingaliv are other popular alternatives to learn more about the Viking age in Stockholm.

39. STAY ACTIVE

Stockholm is a beautiful city, there is no denying that. But sometimes you may get sick and tired of being around the hustle and bustle of the Swedish capital.

Hiking is somewhat of an unknown quantity with visitors more likely to want to spend the entirety on their stay exploring but to see the true beauty of Sweden, you need to get outdoors and explore the wilderness. Best of all, most hiking destinations can be easily reached through public transport.

Located close to the capital, Tyresta National Park offers beautiful lakes and nearly 5000 acres of primeval pine forests, exactly what an untamed wilderness should feel like.

Graded as a national park in 1993, Tyresta is 20km south of Stockholm's city center. It's one of the largest old-growth forests in southern Sweden, and some of the pine trees here date back from around 400 years ago.

You can spend a full day hiking, spotting wildlife in Tyresta, or grab lunch. Stop by the visitor's center for information or to plan your overnight stay at one of the park's campsites.

Take bus 834 from Haninge train station to Tyrestaby, or alternatively take bus 807 or 809 from Gullmarsplan to Svartbäcken

Additionally, Brunnsviken is a picturesque lake only a short journey away from the north of Stockholm's city center. It's a popular choice for picnicking among families, but it also provides a great opportunity to go for a relaxing walk while also seeing some unusual sights at the same time.

>TOURIST

These grounds makes an ideal escape from the bustle of the city, and hikers can take advantage of a 12km-long trail that makes a scenic loop around the whole area. There are plenty of places to stop and recharge along the way, especially during the summer. Best of all, there is no cover charge.

There are various ways to get to Brunnsviken. The most simple is to take the commuter train to Ulriksdal.

40. WINTER FUN

When most people think of Stockholm and Sweden, the first thing that comes to mind is the cold weather and snow. Both of these things are accurate and the winters are cold, too cold for those of us that are used to single digit winters. The weather drops below 0 degrees Celsius and is consistently between -5 and -15 degrees Celsius between December and February.

Along with this, there isn't much daylight during these months with the shortest day of the year in January seeing five hours of light (not much of it.) However, it isn't all bad news as winter also brings a lot of fun activities such as the Christmas Markets throughout December.

Hammarbybacken is a hotspot for locals and tourists alike during the winter season. Here you will find a snow park with numerous slopes to snowboard or ski. There are hotels as well where you can rent equipment, enjoy the cafes and restaurants. The ski resort offers an incredible experience for all ages and skill levels, while enjoying an astounding view of the city. Once you have finished skiing for the day, you can settle down with a fika, which will warm you up after a day on the slopes.

Vasaparken plays host to one of Stockholm's best outdoor ice rinks with long opening hours (8:00-21:00 on weekdays and 10:00-21:00 on weekends.) It is in operation from November right up to March. When the park is lit up it's a magical place to skate.

Be sure to pack your waterproof boots, thermal base layers and knitted hat and gloves if you are arriving in Stockholm in the winter, they will be needed.

>TOURIST

41. NEED TO WORK?

The co-working scene in Stockholm is booming right now and this will only continue to get bigger and better. There is now a variety of options with regards to sharing workspaces whether you are a freelancer or entrepreneur. They are all different, so your own preference will ultimately decide which one is perfect for you.

Whether you are looking for a simple cafe with internet connection or an elaborate office space with extra perks such as balconies, I have put together some of the options you should consider.

Convendum is one of the most modern co-working spaces that you will find in the entire city. Based one minute away from the T-Centralen, it is ideal for everyone to get to. There are also other spaces located around the city but this is my personal preference. There are also options for lockable office and conference rooms if that is what you are looking for. The space is elegant and luxurious, with 24-7 hour access for members.

As you can imagine, there is a wide range of benefits for using this co-working space, after all it is priced within the higher end of options.

Telefonplan is one of the up-and-coming neighborhoods in the city and Kolonien's working space offers one of the best priced office spots in Stockholm. Kolonien is based in an office hotel, where professional freelancers and companies come to rent desktops or private office spaces. It is perfect whether you are working individually or as part of a team, short term or on a longer project, they cover every base.

The Castle's co-working space located in Gamla Stan offers five floors of working space. There is over 1500 square meters shared by over 200 people who believe that a workspace can be more than just a regular office. The Castle aims to create the workspace of dreams through a culture and community that can't be matched anywhere else in Stockholm.

>TOURIST
42. SPORT IN STOCKHOLM

The biggest sport in Sweden is Ice Hockey, with fixtures in Stockholm must-see. Away from their North American rivals Sweden are the next best in the hockey world, while the SHL is among the most competitive and high quality hockey in the world.

The most prominent clubs in Stockholm are Djurgården and AIK. The hockey season starts in September and ends in March. Tickets can be bought either at the arena on game day, through the different clubs' web pages.

Derbies from around the soccer world are nothing new, but in Stockholm- they have one of fiercest rivalries in world soccer. Many Stockholm football fans often clash when it comes to 'the' derby. There are three teams based around Stockholm with all classing a different part of the city as theirs.

Djurgården Fans call themselves the Djurgårdare, the Östermalm district is considered the home of the side. This is because Djurgården's former home ground Stadion is situated here. Whereas, AIK have their spiritual home in Solna and Hammarby in Södermalm.

Meanwhile, there are a few more unusual sports that are played in Sweden. Bandy is one of which and is a long serving Swedish tradition that they always achieve great success when competing on the world stage.

It is the second most popular ice-based sport (after ice skating) and it is easiest described as a mixture of hockey and association football.

Floorball is another form of hockey, this time it is played indoors. It is contested between two teams, consisting of five outfield players and one goalkeeper. Floorball is played with a small plastic ball with holes in it and there are three twenty minute periods; as there are in ice hockey. The sport is still relatively new having only been formed in 1970 in Gothenburg; this is reflected in the fact that there are only 4,330 clubs worldwide. It is however, a very fun sport to watch so catch a game if you can.

>TOURIST

43. SMART CASUAL

Stockholm is a very snazzy location for a weekend or a longer break, it is that cool that there really is no rules when it comes to how you dress. In most European cities when a nightclub or restaurant says to dress smart, you will be expected to wear a suit complete with a tie. That is not the case in Stockholm- in fact it's very rare you see anybody wearing a suit.

Smart in Stockholm, generally means 'smart casual', and by that term they mean jeans with a polo shirt or shirt. It doesn't necessarily mean that you have to wear a suit jacket or tie. This is even the case with work clothing. On my first day of work in the city, I wore a suit only to be told within minutes that there is no need to wear a suit to work at all. My bosses said that as long as the clothing that was worn was comfy, that is when your work will excel the most. Something that was so clearly true.

This also transcends to life outside of work, it's very rare that you see women is dresses or men in dinner suits- unless they are attending a wedding.

44. ISLAND HOPPING

One of the many ways to experience the Stockholm archipelago is to travel by ferry from island to island. Lapping waves and beautiful scenery awaits you. Boats all year round and is the perfect way to see Stockholm; it's my favorite.

When buying a ticket or pass, ask for a Waxholmsbolaget's island hopping map. It has suggestions for different routes and things to do along the way. The area is divided into the northern, central, and southern archipelago. You can download Waxholmsbolaget's app (simply search for 'Waxholmsbolaget') and use it to plan your journey.

There are many different lodging options on the islands. Camp, stay at hostels or check into hotels. Make reservations well in advance during high season.

For those only making a few trips, single tickets are recommended. Ticket prices vary according to route from 50 SEK to 150 SEK. An island hopping pass is good for five days and costs SEK 420. Just be sure to bring warm clothes and mosquito repellant for a hot day.

>TOURIST

45. LUNCH MEAL HACKS

Stockholm's restaurant scene has a reputation for being outlandishly expensive. Unfortunately, I'm not here to dispel that rumor today, but rather to offer a more affordable alternative.

Sit down for a proper restaurant meal and your wallet is bound to feel the pinch, but dine al fresco at one of the city's kiosks and save. Hot dog kiosks are easily the most popular (korv in Swedish) but other options (like Thai takeaways) do exist.

Or if you're in the mood for a burger, hit up the local fast food chain, Max. A regular burger (albeit a small one) costs just 15 SEK ($1.76) without add-ons.

Research is the key, you will find the ideal place for lunch but I would stay well clear of Östermalm- even the pop-up kiosks are expensive in that area.

Gamla Stan restaurants have a special lunch menu. Usually, it's around 100 SEK. For this you get one dish and the Swedish favorite of a self-serving salad bar. It is a substantial meal that would easily sustain you through a business day. Naturally, you do not need to work in the Old Town – restaurants would gladly serve it to hungry tourists or anybody who happened to wander on their premises around noon.

46. SKYVIEW ELEVATOR

This unique attraction transports tourists to the top of the world's largest spherical building, Ericsson Globe. Additionally, SkyView is completely accessible to wheelchairs.

Ericsson Globe, known by locals as simply Globen ("The Globe"), is a massive indoor arena in Sweden's capital city. The Globe has hosted all manner of events, including music concerts, award shows and sporting contests. The first two games of the 2008-09 NHL season were played abroad - in The Globe.

The structure, holding the record of largest hemispherical building in the world, was opened in 1989. Its interior volume exceeds 21 million cubic feet, with an indoor height of 279 feet.

>TOURIST

SkyView Stockholm is an attraction connected to, but separate from the Globe. It is aimed at tourists visiting the City of Stockholm. SkyView consists of two spherical inclined elevators that run on tracks attached to the exterior of the Ericsson Globe. Each "carriage" holds up to 20 people and provides an elevated view of the city's skyline. I like to think of it as a sightseeing funicular that climbs a building, rather than a hill. It reaches the apex of the building at a height of 425 feet.

The entire experience lasts around 30 minutes, so it doesn't require much of a time commitment and is definitely something to do if you have spare time.

47. SEA FOOD LOVERS

If you are a lover of sea food, Stockholm is the place for you and you will never want to leave.

This is the one cuisine Stockholm does quite well alongside traditional Swedish dishes. The city's proximity to the Baltic Sea and centuries of fishing out their daily sustenance from the Atlantic Ocean, North Sea, and Baltic Sea means Swedes have mastered the art of cooking seafood, but more importantly, have uncovered the true versatility of fish.

In the Nordics, it's mostly all types of fresh fish and baby prawns, crawfish and fish roe, and all manner of smoked fish. Yes, you'll still find larger shellfish and mollusks in a few restaurants but they're far and few in-between.

Herring is an integral part of Nordic culture. Known as Sill in Swedish, there are 15 species of this silver colored fish worldwide. Chances are you'll be eating either Atlantic or Baltic herring in Sweden.

When in doubt, it never hurts to fall back onto salmon. Even better if you try traditional cured salmon (gravad lax or gravlax), which is usually served cold. You really can't go wrong with any fish you order off a menu but if you happen to see Arctic Char listed, forget the other options and order this one. Similar to salmon in terms of being from the same family and having the same consistency, Arctic char is a cold-water fish which has lighter colored flesh and is usually served pan-seared. A favorite among locals and you'll understand why once you try it.

>TOURIST

48. APPROPRIATE FOOTWEAR

This is a pretty big one. The public transport- as I have previously mentioned- is excellent and a great way to get around. However, the best way to truly experience a city is on foot. Stockholm is large and that in turn means that there will be a lot of walking- good and comfy walking shoes are a must.

Also, due to the cobbled streets around Gamla Stan, I would say to stay well clear of wearing heels if you have plans to go around the famous old streets.

Meanwhile, if you're planning a winter trip, bring along some very sturdy shoes. From November through till March you can expect the ground to be covered in 'slask.' This is simply an uncomfortable and slippery mix of melted snow and grit. It keeps you from falling over, but it will leave its mark on your footwear.

49. ATTENDING A WEEKEND HOUSE PARTY?

Buying alcohol in Sweden is a bit of a nightmare, this is something that still takes me by surprise every weekend.

The Swedish government has a monopoly on alcohol—if it's over 3.5% ABV, anyway. For the strong stuff, you'll need to head to government-owned Systembolaget, which close early afternoons on Saturday and don't open at all on Sundays.

If you would prefer a 2% beer- affectionately known to locals as folköl, or 'the people's beer'- you can get these in any regular store.

This is easily the most affordable way to drink in Sweden–a nice imported beer might cost you 25 SEK ($2.93) here, whereas the same beer can cost 80 SEK ($9.37) in a bar.

>TOURIST

50. DO THE FREE WALKING TOUR

It's true, there are a few free things to do in Stockholm, and a free walking tour is one of them. I would recommend doing all the free things in Stockholm as they are all something that you would happily pay for once you have finished. The walking tour could be the pick of the bunch and is the perfect city experience.

The tours are available in English and Spanish and will take you to the main sites of the capital. Tours start daily at 10 am in Gamla Stan and last for about 1 hour and 30 minutes.

Of course, as with any other "free" tour, gratuity is appreciated by your guide, but the price is up to you. These tours run all year, just make sure to dress appropriately for the weather. The best options are Stockholm Free Tours or Free Walking Tour Stockholm.

As always, check the company's website for the full schedules.

>TOURIST
TOP REASONS TO BOOK THIS TRIP

History: The history of Sweden and the Vikings is unparallel and you will find yourself gripped, wanting to know more.

Locals: Swedes are brilliant and once you have broken the uncomfortable nervousness, they are the best nationality of people. After all, it's the people that make the trip perfect.

Scenery: It is beautiful and has to be seen to be believed. Every angle of the city is picturesque.

\>TOURIST
RESOURCES

https://www.visitstockholm.com/

https://www.lonelyplanet.com/sweden/stockholm

https://www.tripadvisor.com/Tourism-g189852-Stockholm-Vacations.html

https://www.planetware.com/tourist-attractions-/stockholm-s-upp-stock.htm

https://www.travelandleisure.com/travel-guide/stockholm-sweden

https://visitsweden.com/stockholm/

https://visitsweden.com/sweden-facts/

https://www.lonelyplanet.com/maps/europe/sweden/stockholm/

http://www.orangesmile.com/travelguide/stockholm/city-maps.htm

https://www.routesnorth.com/

https://www.slowtravelstockholm.com/

https://www.nordicvisitor.com/

https://www.scandinaviantravel.com/

https://sl.se/en/fares--tickets/

https://www.accuweather.com/en/se/stockholm/314929/weather-forecast/314929

https://www.stockholmpass.com/

https://international.stockholm.se/

https://www.stockholmarchipelago.se/en/

https://transportstyrelsen.se/en/road/Congestion-taxes-in-Stockholm-and-Goteborg/

>TOURIST

BONUS BOOK

50 THINGS TO KNOW ABOUT PACKING LIGHT FOR TRAVEL

PACK THE RIGHT WAY EVERY TIME

AUTHOR: MANIDIPA BHATTACHARYYA

First Published in 2015 by Dr. Lisa Rusczyk. Copyright 2015. All Rights Reserved. No part of this publication may be reproduced, including scanning and photocopying, or distributed in any form or by any means, electronic or mechanical, or stored in a database or retrieval system without prior written permission from the publisher.

Disclaimer: The publisher has put forth an effort in preparing and arranging this book. The information provided herein by the author is provided "as is". Use this information at your own risk. The publisher is not a licensed doctor. Consult your doctor before engaging in any medical activities. The publisher and author disclaim any liabilities for any loss of profit or commercial or personal damages resulting from the information contained in this book.

Edited by Melanie Howthorne

ABOUT THE AUTHOR

Manidipa Bhattacharyya is a creative writer and editor, with an education in English literature and Linguistics. After working in the IT industry for seven long years she decided to call it quits and follow her heart instead. Manidipa has been ghost writing, editing, proof reading and doing secondary research services for many story tellers and article writers for about three years. She stays in Kolkata, India with her husband and a busy two year old. In her own time Manidipa enjoys travelling, photography and writing flash fiction.

Manidipa believes in travelling light and never carries anything that she couldn't haul herself on a trip. However, travelling with her child changed the scenario. She seemed to carry the entire world with her for the baby on the first two trips. But good sense prevailed and she is again working her way to becoming a light traveler, this time with a kid.

>TOURIST

INTRODUCTION

He who would travel happily must travel light.

-Antoine de Saint-Exupéry

Travel takes you to different places from seas and mountains to deserts and much more. In your travels you get to interact with different people and their cultures. You will, however, enjoy the sights and interact positively with these new people even more, if you are travelling light.

When you travel light your mind can be free from worry about your belongings. You do not have to spend precious vacation time waiting for your luggage to arrive after a long flight. There is be no chance of your bags going missing and the best part is that you need not pay a fee for checked baggage.

People who have mastered this art of packing light will root for you to take only one carry-on, wherever you go. However, many people can find it really hard to pack light. More so if you are travelling with children. Differentiating between "must have" and "just in case" items is the starting point. There will be ample shopping avenues at your destination which are just waiting to be explored.

This book will show you 'packing' in a new 'light' – pun intended – and help you to embrace light packing practices for all of your future travels.

Off to packing!

DEDICATION

I dedicate this book to all the travel buffs that I know, who have given me great insights into the contents of their backpacks.

THE RIGHT TRAVEL GEAR

1. CHOOSE YOUR TRAVEL GEAR CAREFULLY

While selecting your travel gear, pick items that are light weight, durable and most importantly, easy to carry. There are cases with wheels so you can drag them along – these are usually on the heavy side because of the trolley. Alternatively a backpack that you can carry comfortably on your back, or even a duffel bag that you can carry easily by hand or sling across your body are also great options. Whatever you choose, one thing to keep in mind is that the luggage itself should not weigh a ton, this will give you the flexibility to bring along one extra pair of shoes if you so desire.

>TOURIST

2. CARRY THE MINIMUM NUMBER OF BAGS

Selecting light weight luggage is not everything. You need to restrict the number of bags you carry as well. One carry-on size bag is ideal for light travel. Most carriers allow one cabin baggage plus one purse, handbag or camera bag as long as it slides under the seat in front. So technically, you can carry two items of luggage without checking them in.

3. PACK ONE EXTRA BAG

Always pack one extra empty bag along with your essential items. This could be a very light weight duffel bag or even a sturdy tote bag which takes up minimal space. In the event that you end up buying a lot of souvenirs, you already have a handy bag to stuff all that into and do not have to spend time hunting for an appropriate bag.

> *I'm very strict with my packing and have everything in its right place. I never change a rule. I hardly use anything in the hotel room. I wheel my own wardrobe in and that's it.*

Charlie Watts

CLOTHES & ACCESSORIES

4. PLAN AHEAD

Figure out in advance what you plan to do on your trip. That will help you to pick that one dress you need for the occasion. If you are going to attend a wedding then you have to carry formal wear. If not, you can ditch the gown for something lighter that will be comfortable during long walks or on the beach.

5. WEAR THAT JACKET

Remember that wearing items will not add extra luggage for your air travel. So wear that bulky jacket that you plan to carry for your trip. This saves space and can also help keep you warm during the chilly flight.

6. MIX AND MATCH

Carry clothes that can be interchangeably used to reinvent your look. Find one top that goes well with a couple of pairs of pants or skirts. Use tops, shirts and jackets wisely along with other accessories like a scarf or a stole to create a new look.

>TOURIST

7. CHOOSE YOUR FABRIC WISELY

Stuffing clothes in cramped bags definitely takes its toll which results in wrinkles. It is best to carry wrinkle free, synthetic clothes or merino tops. This will eliminate the need for that small iron you usually bring along.

8. DITCH CLOTHES PACK UNDERWEAR

Pack more underwear and socks. These are the things that will give you a fresh feel even if you do not get a chance to wear fresh clothes. Moreover these are easy to wash and can be dried inside the hotel room itself.

9. CHOOSE DARK OVER LIGHT

While picking your clothes choose dark coloured ones. They are easy to colour coordinate and can last longer before needing a wash. Accidental food spills and dirt from the road are less visible on darker clothes.

10. WEAR YOUR JEANS

Take only one pair of Jeans with you, which you should wear on the flight. Remember to pick a pair that can be worn for sightseeing trips and is equally eloquent for dinner. You can add variety by adding light weight cargoes and chinos.

11. CARRY SMART ACCESSORIES

The right accessory can give you a fresh look even with the same old dress. An intelligent neck-piece, a couple of bright scarves, stoles or a sarong can be used in a number of ways to add variety to your clothing. These light weight beauties can double up as a nursing cover, a light blanket, beach wear, a modesty cover for visiting places of worship, and also makes for an enthralling game of peek-a-boo.

12. LEARN TO FOLD YOUR GARMENTS

Seasoned travellers all swear by rolling their clothes for compact and wrinkle free packing. Bundle packing, where you roll the clothes around a central object as if tying it up, is also a popular method of compact and wrinkle free packing. Stacking folded clothes one on top of another is a big no-no as it makes creases extreme and they are difficult to get rid of without ironing.

>TOURIST

13. WASH YOUR DIRTY LAUNDRY

One of the ways to avoid carrying loads of clothes is to wash the clothes you carry. At some places you might get to use the laundry services or a Laundromat but if you are in a pinch, best solution is to wash them yourself. If that is the plan then carrying quick drying clothes is highly recommended, which most often also happen to be the wrinkle free variety.

14. LEAVE THOSE TOWELS BEHIND

Regular towels take up a lot of space, are heavy and take ages to dry out. If you are staying at hotels they will provide you with towels anyway. If you are travelling to a remote place, where the availability of towels look doubtful, carry a light weight travel towel of viscose material to do the job.

15. USE A COMPRESSION BAG

Compression bags are getting lots of recommendation now days from regular travellers. These are useful for saving space in your luggage when you have to pack bulky dresses. While packing for the return trip, get help from the hotel staff to arrange a vacuum cleaner.

FOOTWEAR

16. PUT ON YOUR HIKING BOOTS

If you have plans to go hiking or trekking during your trip, you will need those bulky hiking boots. The best way to carry them is to wear them on flight to save space and luggage weight. You can remove the boots once inside and be comfortable in your socks.

17. PICKING THE RIGHT SHOES

Shoes are often the bulkiest items, along with being the dainty if you are a female. They need care and take up a lot of space in your luggage. It is advisable therefore to pick shoes very carefully. If you plan to do a lot of walking and site seeing, then wearing a pair of comfortable walking shoes are a must. For more formal occasions you can carry durable, light weight flats which will not take up much space.

18. STUFF SHOES

If you happen to pack a pair of shoes, ensure you utilize their hollow insides. Tuck small items like rolled up socks or belts to save space. They will also be easy to find.

\>TOURIST

TOILETRIES

19. STASHING TOILETRIES

Carry only absolute necessities. Airline rules dictate that for one carry-on bag, liquids and gels must be in 3.4 ounce (100ml) bottles or less, and must be packed in a one quart zip-lock bag. If you are planning to stay in a hotel, the basic things will be provided for you. It's best is to buy the rest from the local market at your destination.

20. TAKE ALONG TAMPONS

Tampons are a hard to find item in a lot of countries. Figure out how many you need and pack accordingly. For longer stays you can buy them online and have them delivered to where you are staying.

21. GET PAMPERED BEFORE YOU TRAVEL

Some avid travellers suggest getting a pedicure and manicure just the day before travelling. This not only gives you a well kept look, you also save the trouble of packing nail polish. Remember, every little bit of weight reduced adds up.

ELECTRONICS

22. LUGGING ALONG ELECTRONICS

Electronics have a large role to play in our lives today. Most of us cannot imagine our lives away from our phones, laptops or tablets. However while travelling, one must consider the amount of weight these electronics add to our luggage. Thankfully smart phones come along with all the essentials tools like a camera, email access, picture editing tools and more. They are smart to the point of eliminating the need to carry multiple gadgets. Choose a smart phone that suits all your requirements and travel with the world in your palms or pocket.

23. REDUCE THE NUMBER OF CHARGERS

If you do travel with multiple electronic devices, you will have to bear the additional burden of carrying all their chargers too. Check if a single charger can be used for multiple devices. You might also consider investing in a pocket charger. These small devices support multiple devices while keeping you charged on the go.

>TOURIST

24. TRAVEL FRIENDLY APPS

Along with smart phones come numerous apps, which are immensely helpful in our travels. You name it and you have an app for it at hand – take pictures, sharing with friends and family, torch to light dark roads, maps, checking flight/train times, find hotels and many other things. Use these smart alternatives to traditional items like books to eliminate weight and save space.

> *I get ideas about what's essential when packing my suitcase.*

-Diane von Furstenberg

TRAVELLING WITH KIDS

25. BRING ALONG THE STROLLER

Kids might enjoy walking for a while but they soon tire out and a stroller is the just the right thing for them to rest in while you continue your tour. Strollers also double duty as a luggage carrier and shopping bag holder. Remember to pick a light weight, easy to handle brand of stroller. Better yet, find out in advance if you can rent a stroller at your destination.

26. BRING ONLY ENOUGH DIAPERS FOR YOUR TRIP

Diapers take up a lot of space and add to the weight of your luggage. Therefore it is advisable to carry just enough diapers to last through the trip and a few for afterwards, till you buy fresh stock at your destination. Unless of course you are travelling to a really remote area, in which case you have no choice but to carry the load. Otherwise diapers are something you will find pretty easily.

27. TAKE ONLY A COUPLE OF TOYS

Children are easily attracted by new things in their environment. While travelling they will find numerous 'new' objects to scrutinize and play with. Packing just one favorite toy is enough, or if there is no favorite toy leave out all of them in favor of stories or imaginary games.

28. CARRY KID FRIENDLY SNACKS

Create a small snack counter in your bag to store away quick bites for those sudden hunger pangs. Depending on the child's age this could include chocolates, raisins, dry fruits, granola bars or biscuits. Also keep a bottle of water handy for your little one.

These things do not add much weight and can be adjusted in a handbag or knapsack.

29. GAMES TO CARRY

Create some travel specific, imaginary games if you have slightly grown up children, like spot the attractions. Keep a coloring book and colors handy for in-flight or hotel time. Apps on your smart phone can keep the children engaged with cartoons and story books. Older children are often entertained by games available on phones or tablets. This cuts the weight of luggage down while keeping the kids entertained.

30. LET THE KIDS CARRY THEIR LOAD

A good thing is to start early sharing of responsibilities. Let your child pick a bag of his or her choice and pack it themselves. Keep tabs on what they are stuffing in their bags by asking if they will be using that item on the trip. It could start out being just an entertainment bag initially but with growing years they will learn to sort the useful from the superfluous. Children as little as four can maneuver a small trolley suitcase like a pro- their experience in pull along toys credit. If you are worried that you may be pulling it for them, you may want to start with a backpack.

31. DECIDE ON LOCATION FOR CHILDREN TO SLEEP

While on a trip you might not always get a crib at your destination, and carrying one will make life all the more difficult. Instead call ahead to see if there are any cribs or roll out beds for children. You may even put blankets on the floor. Weave them a story about camping and they will gladly sleep without any trouble.

32. GET BABY PRODUCTS DELIVERED AT YOUR DESTINATION

If you are absolutely paranoid about not getting your favourite variety of diaper or brand of baby food, check out online stores like amazon.com for services in your destination city. You can buy things online ahead of your travel and get them delivered to your hotel upon arrival.

33. FEEDING NEEDS OF YOUR INFANTS

If you are travelling with a breastfed infant, you save the trouble of carrying bottles and bottle sanitization kits. For special food, or medications, you may need to call ahead to make sure you have a refrigerator where you are staying.

34. FEEDING NEEDS OF YOUR TODDLER

With the progression from infancy to toddler, their dietary requirements too evolve. You will have to pack some snacks for travelling time. Fresh fruits and vegetables can be purchased at your destination. Most of the cities you travel to in whichever part of the world, will have baby food products and formulas, available at the local drug-store or the supermarket.

35. PICKING CLOTHES FOR YOUR BABY

Contrary to popular belief, babies can do without many changes of clothes. At the most pack 2 outfits per day. Pack mix and match type clothes for your little one as well. Pick things which are comfortable to wear and quick to dry.

36. SELECTING SHOES FOR YOUR BABY

Like outfits, kids can make do with two pairs of comfortable shoes. If you can get some water resistant shoes it will be best. To expedite drying wet shoes, you can stuff newspaper in them then wrap them with newspaper and leave them to dry overnight.

37. KEEP ONE CHANGE OF CLOTHES HANDY

Travelling with kids can be tricky. Keep a change of clothes for the kids and mum handy in your purse or tote bag. This takes a bit of space in your hand luggage but comes extremely handy in case there are any accidents or spills.

38. LEAVE BEHIND BABY ACCESSORIES

Baby accessories like their bed, bath tub, car seat, crib etc. should be left at home. Many hotels provide a crib on request, while car seats can be borrowed from friends or rented. Babies can be given a bath in the hotel sink or even in the adult bath tub with a little bit of water. If you bring a few bath toys, they can be used in the bath, pool, and out of water. They can also be sanitized easily in the sink.

39. CARRY A SMALL LOAD OF PLASTIC BAGS

With children around there are chances of a number of soiled clothes and diapers. These plastic bags help to sort the dirt from the clean inside your big bag.

These are very light weight and come in handy to other carry stuff as well at times.

PACK WITH A PURPOSE

40. PACKING FOR BUSINESS TRIPS

One neutral-colored suit should suffice. It can be paired with different shirts, ties and accessories for different occasions. One pair of black suit pants could be worn with a matching jacket for the office or with a snazzy top for dinner.

41. PACKING FOR A CRUISE

Most cruises have formal dinners, and that formal dress usually takes up a lot of space. However you might find a tuxedo to rent. For women, a short black dress with multiple accessory options will do the trick.

42. PACKING FOR A LONG TRIP OVER DIFFERENT CLIMATES

The secret packing mantra for travel over multiple climates is layering. Layering traps air around your body creating insulation against the cold. The same light t-shirt that is comfortable in a warmer climate can be the innermost layer in a colder climate.

REDUCE SOME MORE WEIGHT

43. LEAVE PRECIOUS THINGS AT HOME

Things that you would hate to lose or get damaged leave them at home. Precious jewelry, expensive gadgets or dresses, could be anything. You will not require these on your trip. Leave them at home and spare the load on your mind.

44. SEND SOUVENIRS BY MAIL

If you have spent all your money on purchasing souvenirs, carrying them back in the same bag that you brought along would be difficult. Either pack everything in another bag and check it in the airport or get everything shipped to your home. Use an international carrier for a secure transit, but this could be more expensive than the checking fees at the airport.

45. AVOID CARRYING BOOKS

Books equal to weight. There are many reading apps which you can download on your smart phone or tab.

Plus there are gadgets like Kindle and Nook that are thinner and lighter alternatives to your regular book.

CHECK, GET, SET, CHECK AGAIN

46. STRATEGIZE BEFORE PACKING

Create a travel list and prepare all that you think you need to carry along. Keep everything on your bed or floor before packing and then think through once again – do I really need that? Any item that meets this question can be avoided. Remove whatever you don't really need and pack the rest.

47. TEST YOUR LUGGAGE

Once you have fully packed for the trip take a test trip with your luggage. Take your bags and go to town for window shopping for an hour. If you enjoy your hour long trip it is good to go, if not, go home and reduce the load some more. Repeat this test till you hit the right weight.

48. ADD A ROLL OF DUCT TAPE

You might wonder why, when this book has been talking about reducing stuff, we're suddenly asking you to pack something totally unusual. This is because when you have limited supplies, duct tape is immensely helpful for small repairs – a broken bag, leaking zip-lock bag, broken sunglasses, you name it and duct tape can fix it, temporarily.

49. LIST OF ESSENTIAL ITEMS

Even though the emphasis is on packing light, there are things which have to be carried for any trip. Here is our list of essentials:

- Passport/Visa or any other ID

- Any other paper work that might be required on a trip like permits, hotel reservation confirmations etc.

- Medicines – all your prescription medicines and emergency kit, especially if you are travelling with children

- Medical or vaccination records

- Money in foreign currency if travelling to a different country

- Tickets- Email or Message them to your phone

>TOURIST

50. MAKE THE MOST OF YOUR TRIP

Wherever you are going, whatever you hope to do we encourage you to embrace it whole-heartedly. Take in the scenery, the culture and above all, enjoy your time away from home.

On a long journey even a straw weighs heavy.

-Spanish Proverb

>TOURIST

PACKING AND PLANNING TIPS

A Week before Leaving

- Arrange for someone to take care of pets and water plants.
- Stop mail and newspaper.
- Notify Credit Card companies where you are going.
- Change your thermostat settings.
- Car inspected, oil is changed, and tires have the correct pressure.
- Passports and photo identification is up to date.
- Pay bills.
- Copy important items and download travel Apps.
- Start collecting small bills for tips.

Right Before Leaving

- Clean out refrigerator.
- Empty garbage cans.
- Lock windows.
- Make sure you have the proper identification with you.
- Bring cash for tips.
- Remember travel documents.
- Lock door behind you.
- Remember wallet.
- Unplug items in house and pack chargers.

>TOURIST

READ OTHER GREATER THAN A TOURIST BOOKS

Greater Than a Tourist San Miguel de Allende Guanajuato Mexico: 50 Travel Tips from a Local by Tom Peterson

Greater Than a Tourist – Lake George Area New York USA: 50 Travel Tips from a Local by Janine Hirschklau

Greater Than a Tourist – Monterey California United States: 50 Travel Tips from a Local by Katie Begley

Greater Than a Tourist – Chanai Crete Greece: 50 Travel Tips from a Local by Dimitra Papagrigoraki

Greater Than a Tourist – The Garden Route Western Cape Province South Africa: 50 Travel Tips from a Local by Li-Anne McGregor van Aardt

Greater Than a Tourist – Sevilla Andalusia Spain: 50 Travel Tips from a Local by Gabi Gazon

Greater Than a Tourist – Kota Bharu Kelantan Malaysia: 50 Travel Tips from a Local by Aditi Shukla

Children's Book: Charlie the Cavalier Travels the World by Lisa Rusczyk

>TOURIST

> TOURIST

Visit Greater Than a Tourist for Free Travel Tips
http://GreaterThanATourist.com

Sign up for the Greater Than a Tourist Newsletter for discount days, new books, and travel information:
http://eepurl.com/cxspyf

Follow us on Facebook for tips, images, and ideas:
https://www.facebook.com/GreaterThanATourist

Follow us on Pinterest for travel tips and ideas:
http://pinterest.com/GreaterThanATourist

Follow us on Instagram for beautiful travel images:
http://Instagram.com/GreaterThanATourist

>TOURIST

> TOURIST

Please leave your honest review of this book on Amazon and Goodreads. Please send your feedback to GreaterThanaTourist@gmail.com as we continue to improve the series. We appreciate your positive and constructive feedback. Thank you.

>TOURIST

METRIC CONVERSIONS

TEMPERATURE

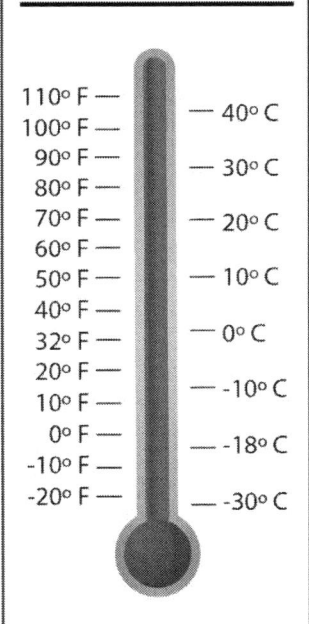

110° F — — 40° C
100° F —
90° F — — 30° C
80° F —
70° F — — 20° C
60° F —
50° F — — 10° C
40° F —
32° F — — 0° C
20° F —
10° F — — -10° C
0° F —
-10° F — — -18° C
-20° F — — -30° C

To convert F to C:
Subtract 32, and then multiply by 5/9 or .5555.

To Convert C to F:
Multiply by 1.8 and then add 32.

32F = 0C

LIQUID VOLUME

To Convert:................Multiply by
U.S. Gallons to Liters................. 3.8
U.S. Liters to Gallons 26
Imperial Gallons to U.S. Gallons 1.2
Imperial Gallons to Liters....... 4.55
Liters to Imperial Gallons 22
1 Liter = .26 U.S. Gallon
1 U.S. Gallon = 3.8 Liters

DISTANCE

To convert ....Multiply by
Inches to Centimeters 2.54
Centimeters to Inches 39
Feet to Meters....................... .3
Meters to Feet 3.28
Yards to Meters 91
Meters to Yards 1.09
Miles to Kilometers 1.61
Kilometers to Miles............. .62
1 Mile = 1.6 km
1 km = .62 Miles

WEIGHT

1 Ounce = .28 Grams
1 Pound = .4555 Kilograms
1 Gram = .04 Ounce
1 Kilogram = 2.2 Pounds

107

\>TOURIST

TRAVEL QUESTIONS

- Do you bring presents home to family or friends after a vacation?
- Do you get motion sick?
- Do you have a favorite billboard?
- Do you know what to do if there is a flat tire?
- Do you like a sun roof open?
- Do you like to eat in the car?
- Do you like to wear sun glasses in the car?
- Do you like toppings on your ice cream?
- Do you use public bathrooms?
- Did you bring your cell phone and does it have power?
- Do you have a form of identification with you?
- Have you ever been pulled over by a cop?
- Have you ever given money to a stranger on a road trip?
- Have you ever taken a road trip with animals?
- Have you ever went on a vacation alone?
- Have you ever run out of gas?

- If you could move to any place in the world, where would it be?
- If you could travel anywhere in the world, where would you travel?
- If you could travel in any vehicle, which one would it be?
- If you had three things to wish for from a magic genie, what would they be?
- If you have a driver's license, how many times did it take you to pass the test?
- What are you the most afraid of on vacation?
- What do you want to get away from the most when you are on vacation?
- What foods smells bad to you?
- What item do you bring on ever trip with you away from home?
- What makes you sleepy?
- What song would you love to hear on the radio when you're cruising on the highway?
- What travel job would you want the least?
- What will you miss most while you are away from home?
- What is something you always wanted to try?

>TOURIST

- What is the best road side attraction that you ever saw?
- What is the farthest distance you ever biked?
- What is the farthest distance you ever walked?
- What is the weirdest thing you needed to buy while on vacation?
- What is your favorite candy?
- What is your favorite color car?
- What is your favorite family vacation?
- What is your favorite food?
- What is your favorite gas station drink or food?
- What is your favorite license plate design?
- What is your favorite restaurant?
- What is your favorite smell?
- What is your favorite song?
- What is your favorite sound that nature makes?
- What is your favorite thing to bring home from a vacation?
- What is your favorite vacation with friends?
- What is your favorite way to relax?

- Where is the farthest place you ever traveled in a car?
- Where is the farthest place you ever went North, South, East and West?
- Where is your favorite place in the world?
- Who is your favorite singer?
- Who taught you how to drive?
- Who will you miss the most while you are away?
- Who if the first person you will contact when you get to your destination?
- Who brought you on your first vacation?
- Who likes to travel the most in your life?
- Would you rather be hot or cold?
- Would you rather drive above, below, or at the speed limited?
- Would you rather drive on a highway or a back road?
- Would you rather go on a train or a boat?
- Would you rather go to the beach or the woods?

>TOURIST

TRAVEL BUCKET LIST

1.

2.

3.

4.

5.

6.

7.

8.

9.

10.

>TOURIST

NOTES

Printed in Great Britain
by Amazon